The PROMISES of SACRED HEART

By Rev. LAWRENCE G. LOVASIK, S.V.D.
Divine Word Missionary

Nihil Obstat: Daniel V. Flynn, J.C.D., *Censor Librorum*
Imprimatur: ✠ James P. Mahoney, D.D., *Vicar General, Archdiocese of New York*

© 1982 by CATHOLIC BOOK PUBLISHING CORP. N.J.   ISBN 978-0-89942-303-6

CPSIA   June 2013   10 9 8 7 6 5 4 3   A/P

Jesus appeared to Saint Margaret Mary

ST. MARGARET MARY

S T. Margaret Mary was born in 1647 in France. She was a cripple, but the Blessed Virgin Mary cured her. To thank God for the cure she promised to give her life to His service. When she was seventeen, Jesus appeared to her just as He was after He was scourged. At once she entered the Order of the Visitation.

2

Sister Margaret Mary loved our Lord in the Blessed Sacrament very much. He showed her His Sacred Heart in four visions. The flames that come forth from His Heart remind us of His burning love for us and His desire that we love Him in return. The crown of thorns around His Heart reminds us of sacrifice to make up for sin.

Jesus made at least **twelve promises** to her telling her how He would help those who honor His Sacred Heart.

Jesus said to her: "Look at this Heart which has loved people so much, and yet they do not want to love Me in return. Through you My divine Heart wishes to spread its love everywhere on earth."

St. Margaret Mary died in 1690. Her feastday is October 16.

The Twelve Promises of

THE SACRED HEART OF JESUS

1. "I will give to My faithful all the graces necessary in their state of life."

2. "I will bring peace to their homes."

3. "I will comfort them in all their sufferings."

4. "I will be their safe refuge against all the snares of their enemies in life, and above all in death."

5. "I will bestow abundant blessings upon all their undertakings."

6. "Sinners shall find in My Heart the source and the infinite ocean of mercy."

7. "Fervent souls shall mount to high perfection."

8. "I will bless every home in which an image of My Heart will be honored."

9. "Tepid souls shall become fervent."

10. "I will give to priests the gift of touching the most hardened hearts."

11. "Those who promote this devotion shall have their names written in My Heart, never to be effaced."

12. "To all who receive Communion on the First Friday of the month, for nine consecutive months, I will grant the grace of final repentance."

1 ST PROMISE —

"I will give to My faithful all the graces necessary in their state of life."

Grace for Daily Living

SACRED Heart of Jesus,
give me all the graces I need in my life.

I believe that at Holy Mass
the graces You gained for me
when You died on the cross
reach my soul, especially in Holy Communion.

Give me Your grace
which is the life of my soul.
That grace will make my soul holy
and pleasing to God.

Give light to my mind and strength to my will
to do good and avoid evil.

I want to confess my sins
and receive You in Holy Communion often.

Sacred Heart of Jesus, I love You!

2ND PROMISE —
"I will bring peace to their homes."

Peace in the Home

SACRED Heart of Jesus,
bring peace to my home.

You told Your Apostles:
"Peace is My farewell to you,
My peace is My gift to you."

Jesus, give peace to our family.
Keep us from offending You by mortal sin.

Fill our hearts with the love
that comes from Your Sacred Heart.

Help us to forgive each other and to live in peace.

May we enjoy Your peace
in our family here on earth,
so that we may be united again in heaven
to be with You forever.

Sacred Heart of Jesus, I love You!

3RD PROMISE —

"I will comfort them in all their sufferings."

Comfort in Sufferings

SACRED Heart of Jesus,
comfort me in all my sufferings.

You know how weak I am
and how often I am afraid.

You invited me to Your Sacred Heart
when You said: "Come to Me,
all you who are weary and find life burdensome,
and I will refresh you.
Take my yoke upon your shoulders and learn
from Me,
for I am gentle and humble of heart.
Your souls will find rest,
for My yoke is easy and my burden light."

I come to You in Holy Communion,
that You may give me strength.

Sacred Heart of Jesus, I love You!

4TH PROMISE —

"I will be their safe refuge against all the snares of their enemies in life, and above all in death."

Refuge in Danger

SACRED Heart of Jesus,
be my refuge against all evil in this world,
but above all at the hour of my death.

Never let me be separated from You by sin.

Help me to fight bravely
when the devil and the bad things of this world
want to keep me from loving You.

I trust in Your strength and Your grace
to keep me close to You.

Help me at the hour of my death,
when I shall need You most.

Sacred Heart of Jesus, I love You!

5TH PROMISE —

"I will bestow abundant blessings upon all their undertakings."

Success in Work

SACRED Heart of Jesus,
I ask Your blessing on all that I do—
my work, my study, my play.

I want to do everything I can to please You
and to give You honor.

Without Your help I can do nothing.
Be close to me and guide me.

I also ask Your blessing
on the work of my father and mother.

Reward them for being so good to me
and for all they do to make me happy.

I offer all my thoughts, words, and deeds
to Your Sacred Heart.

Sacred Heart of Jesus, I love You!

6TH PROMISE —

"Sinners shall find in My Heart the source and the infinite ocean of mercy."

Mercy for Sinners

SACRED Heart of Jesus,
I have often offended You,
but I am really sorry for all my sins,
and I shall try hard not to offend You again.

You promised to forgive sinners.

Forgive me!

I wish to confess my sins
and to receive You in Holy Communion often
that I may receive Your grace
and the help I need to be good and to avoid evil.

I also ask You to have mercy on our family,
because all of us have sometimes displeased You.
Forgive us our sins and keep us close to You.

I also pray for the sinners of the whole world.

Sacred Heart of Jesus, I love You!

7TH PROMISE —

"Fervent souls shall mount to high perfection."

Guide to Holiness

SACRED Heart of Jesus,
give me Your grace,
without which I cannot be holy.

Help me to be poor in spirit,
that I may seek heavenly riches;
to be meek, that I may overcome all anger;
to seek comfort in my sorrows in Your Sacred
   Heart;
to hunger and thirst for holiness
by loving You with all my heart;
to be merciful to my neighbor
that I may receive Your forgiveness;
to be pure of heart,
that I may be loved by You;
to be a peace-maker
by keeping peace with myself and others.

Sacred Heart of Jesus, I love You!

20

8TH PROMISE —

"I will bless every home in which an image of My heart will be honored."

Blessing on the Home

SACRED Heart of Jesus,
bless with peace and happiness
the family which You chose for me on earth.

We wish to dedicate ourselves to You in a special way,
and to honor Your Sacred Heart in our home.

Keep us from danger,
give us help in time of need,
and give us the grace
to be more like Your own Holy family.

Fill our home with Your peace and love
and be the King of our souls.
Keep us from all sin.

May Your Sacred heart live and reign
in our family.

Sacred Heart of Jesus, I love You!

22

9TH PROMISE —

"Tepid souls shall become fervent."

Strength for the Weak

SACRED Heart of Jesus,
do not let me neglect my soul.
Since You died for my soul,
let me do all I can to save it.

Help me to lead a good life
that I may prove that I really love You.
You said: "He who obeys the commandments
he has from Me
is the man who loves Me:
and he who loves Me
will be loved my My Father.
I too will love him and reveal Myself to him."

I love You.
I want to keep Your commandments.

Give me Your love and help me to know You
    better.
May Your Father love me.

Sacred Heart of Jesus, I love You!

10TH PROMISE —

"I will give to priests the gift of touching the most hardened hearts."

Zeal for Priests

SACRED Heart of Jesus,
Eternal High Priest,
pour out the life-giving graces
of Your loving Heart
upon your priests and make them living images
   of You.

Save souls through Your priests.
Give them the special grace of drawing sinners
to Your Sacred Heart,
that they may find forgiveness and salvation.

May Your Kingdom come
to the hearts of all people
through the zealous work of truly saintly priests.

I ask Your blessing upon every priest
who was ever good to me and to our family.

Sacred Heart of Jesus, I love You!

11 TH PROMISE —

"Those who promote this devotion shall have their names written in My Heart, never to be effaced."

Friend to the Devoted

SACRED Heart of Jesus,
write my name in Your Sacred Heart
because I do want to be devoted to You
and make You known and loved still more.

Teach me the way that I may follow You.

Give me deep faith that I may believe in Your
truth.

I want to come to the heavenly Father
through You.

I pray for all those who honor Your Sacred Heart
that they may become Your Apostles
and make You known and loved.

May Your Kingdom come
through their prayers and good example.

Sacred Heart of Jesus, I love You!

12 TH PROMISE —

"To all those who receive Communion on the First Friday of the month, for nine consecutive months, I will grant the grace of final repentance."

Grace at Death

SACRED Heart of Jesus,
help me to prepare for the day of my death and judgment.
I want to use the graces You give me.
Help me always to do what God wants me to do.

You alone can safely lead me to heaven.
I put my whole life into Your hands.
You are my best Friend, and I trust You.

Reward my devotion to Your Sacred Heart
by granting me the grace
to die in the friendship of God
and to save my soul.
I will try to receive Holy Communion often,
especially on the first Friday of every month.

Sacred Heart of Jesus, I love You!

Sacred Heart of Jesus, I believe in Your love for me.

PRAYERS TO THE SACRED HEART

Offering

SACRED Heart of Jesus,
I give myself to You.

I give You my body, my soul,
and all that I do or think or say.
I want my whole life to be an offering to You
to make You known and loved.

I also offer to You our family.
Help us to obey and love You always.
Keep us from all danger of soul and body.
Bless our life together
with Your peace and love.

We hope for the forgiveness of our sins
through Your mercy,
and for the graces we need to save our souls.
Through Holy Communion and prayer,
keep us close to Your Sacred Heart.

Sacred Heart of Jesus,
we believe in Your love for us.
Help us to love You more.

Thanksgiving

SACRED Heart of Jesus,
I thank You for all the blessings
You have given me.

For my mother and father and our family,
I thank You.

For making me a child of God in Baptism,
I thank You.

For letting me belong to Your holy Catholic
  Church,
I thank You.

For all the graces You have given me
to help me to love and serve You,
I thank You.

For all the good things You have given me
during my whole life,
I thank You.

For the heaven you promised me after this life,
I thank You.

Sacred Heart of Jesus, be my love!